CAMBRIDGE LIBRARY COLLECTION

Books of enduring scholarly value

History

The books reissued in this series include accounts of historical events and movements by eye-witnesses and contemporaries, as well as landmark studies that assembled significant source materials or developed new historiographical methods. The series includes work in social, political and military history on a wide range of periods and regions, giving modern scholars ready access to influential publications of the past.

New College, Oxford

Published during the golden decade before the Great War left an indelible mark on fellows and undergraduates alike, *New College, Oxford* (1906) is a sensitive and affectionate history of an ancient institution in a modern world. Himself a fellow of the college, A. O. Prickard conveys the image of an educational family whose purpose rose 'above the needs of the life of its members' in order to make a valuable contribution to both society and scholarship. Keen to promote the college's ongoing relevance in the new century, Prickard does not allow his fascination with its history to degenerate into nostalgia. As the author himself explains, Oxford is 'a place of visions and dreams, which float about, but do not encumber the earnest life of the present'. Such contentions combine with Edmund New's informal sketches to create an informative, picturesque and often surprising account.

T0382286

Cambridge University Press has long been a pioneer in the reissuing of out-of-print titles from its own backlist, producing digital reprints of books that are still sought after by scholars and students but could not be reprinted economically using traditional technology. The Cambridge Library Collection extends this activity to a wider range of books which are still of importance to researchers and professionals, either for the source material they contain, or as landmarks in the history of their academic discipline.

Drawing from the world-renowned collections in the Cambridge University Library, and guided by the advice of experts in each subject area, Cambridge University Press is using state-of-the-art scanning machines in its own Printing House to capture the content of each book selected for inclusion. The files are processed to give a consistently clear, crisp image, and the books finished to the high quality standard for which the Press is recognised around the world. The latest print-on-demand technology ensures that the books will remain available indefinitely, and that orders for single or multiple copies can quickly be supplied.

The Cambridge Library Collection will bring back to life books of enduring scholarly value (including out-of-copyright works originally issued by other publishers) across a wide range of disciplines in the humanities and social sciences and in science and technology.

New College, Oxford

ARTHUR OCTAVIUS PRICKARD

CAMBRIDGE UNIVERSITY PRESS

Cambridge, New York, Melbourne, Madrid, Cape Town, Singapore,
São Paolo, Delhi, Dubai, Tokyo, Mexico City

Published in the United States of America by Cambridge University Press, New York

www.cambridge.org
Information on this title: www.cambridge.org/9781108017961

© in this compilation Cambridge University Press 2010

This edition first published 1906
This digitally printed version 2010

ISBN 978-1-108-01796-1 Paperback

The College

Monographs

THE COLLEGE
MONOGRAPHS
Edited and Illustrated by
EDMUND H. NEW

TRINITY COLLEGE,
CAMBRIDGE
> W. W. ROUSE BALL.

ST. JOHN'S COLLEGE,
CAMBRIDGE
> THE SENIOR BURSAR.

KING'S COLLEGE,
CAMBRIDGE
> C. R. FAY.

MAGDALEN COLLEGE,
OXFORD
> THE PRESIDENT.

NEW COLLEGE,
OXFORD
> A. O. PRICKARD.

MERTON COLLEGE,
OXFORD
> REV. H. J. WHITE.

ENTRANCE *to* NEW COLL:

NEW  COLLEGE

OXFORD

BY

A. O. PRICKARD

LATE FELLOW OF THE COLLEGE

ILLUSTRATED BY

EDMUND H. NEW

1906: LONDON: J. M. DENT & CO.
NEW YORK: E. P. DUTTON & CO.

PREFATORY NOTE

IN preparing these chapters, I have made free use of the complete and learned *History of New College* by Dr. Rashdall and Mr. Rait (London, F. E. Robinson & Co., 1901), to which the reader is referred for fuller information, and for references to the authorities ; also of Mr. T. F. Kirby's *Annals of Winchester College* and *Winchester Scholars*, the *Life of William of Wykeham*, by the late Rev. G. H. Moberly, and the *History of Winchester College*, by Mr. A. F. Leach. A very few statements are based upon oral tradition ; these have been so far as possible verified. I have received kind help from several friends, but am solely responsible for errors or omissions.

A. O. P.

CONTENTS

CHAPTER I

INTRODUCTORY

CHAPTER II

THE FOUNDER

ix

CONTENTS

CONTENTS

CHAPTER III
THE BUILDINGS

CONTENTS

CHAPTER IV

THE UNIVERSITY AND OTHER COLLEGES

CHAPTER V

THE HISTORY OF FIVE HUNDRED YEARS

CONTENTS

CHAPTER VI

THE OLD AND THE NEW

LIST OF ILLUSTRATIONS

The Hall Stairs

E.K.N.

New College

CHAPTER I

INTRODUCTORY

"These old wals, which ye see,
Were first enclosures but of salvage soyle."
—SPENSER.

IT has been said of the colleges of Oxford
that their Statutes are written in stone,
and the remark would be no less true if
made of their history. In a large measure
the same might be said of many great
family houses; we read in their walls a
record of the national struggles which they
have witnessed, and of the gradual changes
in the requirements and ideals of life with
which successive owners have laboured to
keep pace. But a College bears impressed
upon it from its beginning the conscious
idea of a corporate aim, of a purpose rising
above the needs of the life of its members
from day to day. Generations pass, the
standard of material and intellectual life
outside rises, or suffers change; yet the
initial force of the life lived by the first
dwellers in these beautiful homes is never

A

quite lost, only modified and adjusted to new times; and every such adjustment leaves its trace on quadrangles and gardens, in Chapel, Hall, and Library. The group of buildings as they stand at any time is at once a record of the life which has been lived there in the past, and a limitation of the form of life which can be lived in the future.

In no one of the Oxford Colleges is the story written in more legible characters than in New College, or, to write its name in full, " The College of Saint Mary of Winchester in Oxford," the elder and more dignified, if not the more beautiful, member of the double foundation of William of Wykeham, Bishop of Winchester in the fourteenth century. Not only is the scale of the fabric ample and even magnificent, far surpassing anything which preceded it in Oxford, but the original design still governs and predominates the whole; the Founder's College, easily distinguished from later accretions, is with us still, not as a curiosity for the antiquarian or the artist, but a living structure, organised and complete in every detail. The additions which time has demanded are in their several ways dignified, and not, we may hope, altogether unworthy of the place they fill. Let us pass within the gateway, and mentally separate the old from the new, before we attempt a closer view of the several parts.

A visitor enters the Great Quadrangle from the west through the principal gate-

way, which he has reached from the outside
by a lane, probably intended to act as a
barbican or defensive approach, lying between two long blank walls, the one of the
College Cloisters, the other of the Brewery.
Above the gateway he will notice three
figures—the Virgin Mother in the centre,
with the Angel of the Annunciation upon
one side, and the Founder on his knees upon
the other. This arrangement is repeated on
the inside of the entrance-tower, and also on
the muniment-tower. The original College
is before him in all its main features. Over
his head are the lodgings of the Warden, in
modern times expanded into a house which
occupies the whole west side, and which
has been skilfully restored and enlarged
under Mr. Caröe's advice; in front of him
the Library fills the upper part of the
east side, with the Bursary on the ground
floor and a second gateway in the middle;
to the right are living rooms arranged
on staircases; to the left the whole of the
north side is filled by the Chapel and
Hall, the Chapel known by its larger windows, and standing west, not, as at Winchester, east of the Hall, so that no
great east window is possible; it is entered
from the passage at the north-west corner,
which also leads to the Cloisters. The stone
stairs leading up to the Hall, lofty itself
though raised so high above the ground, are
at the north-east corner; and let us mention,
for the designer was not a man to scorn

3

domestic details, that from the Hall another flight of stone stairs leads most conveniently past the Buttery down to the Kitchen.

If we continue our way eastwards through the opposite gateway, where no gate now stands, we have still an original building to

THE BUTTERY STAIRCASE

our left, the old Law Library, with a room below it, both now Common-rooms in the use of the Fellows. Beyond this, all which lies between us and the iron railings of the Garden was added, part in the late seventeenth, part in the early eighteenth century. These additions, and certain

4

other modifications of the older building, to which we shall return, mark the successive steps taken to house the number of persons contemplated by the Founder as inmates, just a hundred including Choristers and others, or at least so many of them as were still lodged within the walls, in accordance with the demands of advancing manners. We have yet to notice a development of another kind.

Entering, but not now lingering in the beautiful garden, a well-loved ornament, which has contributed greatly to the common life, we turn back through the old City Wall, till some thirty years ago the northern boundary of the College, and are confronted by a long and massive pile, which runs east and west, and forms one side of Holywell Street, sinking, east of the central gateway and tower, to a less exorbitant height. A large proportion of the resident members, both Fellows and Undergraduates, live here; and it is needless to say that the great expansion in numbers of modern times was only rendered possible by some such structural development. The blocks were erected at various times, the earliest of them in 1873, under the direction of the late Sir Gilbert Scott, the tower over the gateway, and all which lies to the east of it, under that of Mr. Basil Champneys. Thus the City Wall, long treasured as a venerable relic, and an indispensable feature of the Garden, is now a dividing line between past and present ideas; between the College of a hundred members, who, after deducting non-residents, and also the choristers and some others, barely manned the rooms in the middle of the nineteenth century, and the College of two hundred or more, the majority living within the walls, who make old and new alike so populous, so cheerful, and, let us add, so busy.

For, happily, the dividing line does not divide; the whole area within the College Gates, from east to west, and between Queen's Lane and Holywell, once the City Ditch, is a single whole, in which the stream of life flows on some principle of diffusion, one and homogeneous. So, too, it has been the care of those to whom it fell to direct the necessary changes, to preserve a true continuity with the old order, to give direction to the original impulse, not to create a new one; in the words of one who had much to do with Wykeham's foundations, "to interpret the past to the future in the spirit of the present." How far this has been well and truly effected, it is not for us, but for generations hardly yet in being, to pronounce. As the old poet sang, "The days of the future are the wisest of witnesses."

We will pause at our first point of view, or better, at the corner on its right, the south-west angle of the Great Quadrangle, resting our eyes on the Hall Staircase diagonally opposite, and on the group of buildings of which it is the centre, the Hall lying to its left, the Library to its right, and the massive Muniment-Tower, where archives and treasures are stored, rising above it; and ask who and what manner of man it was to whom we owe this inheritance, and what he intended to bequeath to us.

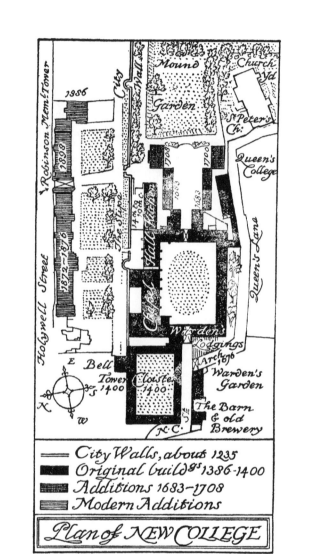

Plan of NEW COLLEGE

CHAPTER II

THE FOUNDER

" The King he sealed the charters, and Wykeham
    traced the plan,
And God, Who gave him wisdom, prospered the
    lowly man."
        —ROUNDELL, EARL OF SELBORNE.

IN the year 1324, the eighteenth of
Edward the Second's unhappy reign,
a son was born to John and Sibill his
wife, both persons of modest station, the
latter at least of gentle lineage, living
at Wykeham, in the valley of the Meon,
between Fareham and Bishops-Waltham
in Hampshire, and received the name of
William. By the help of some unknown
benefactor, probably Sir Ralph Sutton, on
whose behalf he orders a mass to be said
daily in the Chapels of both his Colleges,
naming him next after his own parents, he
received a good education at a school in
Winchester, but did not, it would seem,
pass on to the University. His first appointment was to the office of under-
notary to the Constable of Winchester, by
whom, or by Bishop Edyngton, he was
recommended to Edward III., entering
the royal service at the age of twenty-
three (or perhaps of twenty). In 1356 we
find him at Windsor, with the title of

9

"Surveyor," changed two years later into that of "Surveyor of the Workmen of the King's Castles." The King was at this time full of plans in connection with the new Order of the Garter. The Round Tower had lately been completed, and it was Wykeham's task to adapt and arrange the royal lodgings in the neighbouring part of the structure : we may call attention to the arrangement of a chapel and a hall under one roof, which was afterwards followed in both his Colleges. So far, his employments were entirely of a practical, and, as we should say, a lay kind. Early in life he received his first tonsure, but did not proceed in holy orders for some time, being ordained priest in 1362, in his thirty-eighth year. In the meantime many and rich preferments had accumulated in his hands, irregularly we must allow, and not without protest from Rome. It was at this time that the terrible scourge of the Black Death for the second time devastated England, and other countries of Western Europe ; it had two effects on Wykeham's career, one, that it caused many vacancies in Church preferment, another personal to himself, in turning his thoughts to the means to be taken to replenish the Church ranks ; doubtless also in deepening his own character, as of one whose eye has "kept watch o'er man's mortality" in its most appalling form.

Offices of State now followed, and in

due time the See of Winchester, and the
life of William of Wykeham becomes part
of the history of England. In 1360 he was
with the King at Calais, where the peace
agreed upon at Brétigni, a picturesque incident closing a dreary campaign, was solemnly
ratified ; the articles were drawn, Froissart
tells us, " with great deliberation and much
prudence " ; and, if Wykeham's hand was
in them, it would be in accordance with
his character both as a peacemaker and as
a sagacious counsellor and draftsman. In
1364 he was Keeper of the Privy Seal, and
in 1367 Chancellor. Faithful over castles,
he had become a ruler of kingdoms. " At
that time," says Froissart, "there reigned
a priest in England called Sir William de
Wican, and this Sir William de Wican was
so much in favour with the King of England, that by him everything was done and
without him they did nothing." To all
appearance, it was plain practical ability
which led him to wealth and high office.
In the sense which he himself, according to
a familiar story, quoted, with much hesi-
tation by Bishop Lowth, applied to the
legend inscribed on the walls of Windsor,
" This made Wykeham." But practical
ability alone will not enable a man, when
called to the highest office, to answer to the
call, and bear himself blameless in it ; nor
yet so to use enormous wealth, that he shall
be blessed, not by posterity only, but by his
own dependents and neighbours.

Wykeham's first Chancellorship, 1367–1371, fell in the disastrous time of the re-newed French war, and the last year was

STAIRWAY IN THE WARDEN'S GARDEN

marked by the return of the Black Prince, the people's hope and Wykeham's friend, shattered in health and worn by ill-success

and treachery, to die after lingering five
years in hopeless sickness. The good
Queen Philippa, to whom Wykeham, in a
diocesan letter, pays a touching tribute,
had died in 1369; and the remaining eight
years of the King's reign passed in gloom
and discredit. The Clerical Ministry fell
in consequence of an address to the Crown
from Parliament, praying that "sufficient
and able laymen . . . and no other person,
may be placed in office." Against Wykeham personally the storm, directed by his
persistent enemy, John of Gaunt, Duke of
Lancaster, raged fiercely for many years.
What it concerns us to notice is that, out
of the eight Articles presented against him
to the Council in 1376, only one was
pressed at the hearing. This charged that
the Chancellor had remitted half of a certain
fine due to the King for a licence of feoff-
ment. The answer was that the transac-
tion, which passed in open daylight, was
within the discretion of the Chancellor,
and that the motive was merely charitable.
The charge was held to be proved, and a
fine imposed at the rate of a hundred marks
for every penny lost to the King, making
the huge sum of 960,000 marks. Wykeham was ordered not to approach within
twenty miles of the King's person. So
things passed over the year of the King's
Jubilee, 1377, a melancholy celebration,
where the promise of a renewal of his
grandfather's great reign had once seemed

so brilliant. From the general pardon and grace which marked the occasion Wykeham was excepted by name. But restitution soon followed. On the 18th of June the temporalities of the see were restored to him, on condition of his undertaking certain public charges. On the 21st the King died; at the coronation of Richard Wykeham assisted. In the session of his first Parliament a petition was passed praying that full pardon might be granted to Wykeham, which was at once done, with the full consent of his old enemy, Duke John. He was forthwith taken into the royal employ, and in 1389, when Richard asserted himself against his uncles, he again received the Great Seal. His second Chancellorship fell upon more peaceful times than the first; but it had its own difficulties arising from the young King's uncertain and often unconstitutional demeanour, and from his unfortunate relations with his uncles. In reconciling him to the Duke of Gloucester, Wykeham, to whose gentle and statesman-like mind bygones were bygones, procured the return of the Duke of Lancaster; and a period of strong and fairly representative government followed. Two incidents, showing the constitutional bias of the Chancellor's mind, may be selected for notice. After meeting Parliament in January 1390, he and all the other high officers prayed the King to relieve them of their offices, which was done, and then challenged any complaints. None being forthcoming, and a vote of confidence having been passed, the officers and Council were reinstated, with the inclusion by name of the two Dukes. The other was the framing of a body of by-laws for meetings of the Council, of which No. 1 prescribed the hour of meeting, and the last, No. 14, ran, " When a matter is once entered upon, it shall be finished before any other can be touched "—a sound provision with a pleasantly modern ring ! In 1391 Wykeham resigned the Seal, and put an end to his public life, not, we may believe, fleeing from the evil soon to come, but having done all which prudence could ensure to avert it, and wishing to devote his remaining years, being now near seventy, to the administration of his diocese.

Wykeham had been nominated to the Bishopric of Winchester in 1366, his election by the Chapter of St. Swithun having taken place in October of that year, and having been at once confirmed by the King. Delays had followed, caused by the opposition of the Roman Court ; and it was not till October 1367 that he was consecrated in St. Paul's, nor till July 1368 that he was enthroned. Thus during part of his tenure of the office of Privy Seal, and of his first Chancellorship, he was styled Bishop-Elect of Winchester. The government of his diocese showed the same administrative power which we have seen him exercise in the great offices of State, and an unflinching courage in exposing and rectifying abuses. His Episcopal Register is a perfect record of all business proceedings during his thirty-eight years' tenure of the See; and contains also, as we have already noticed, letters to the diocese on events of public interest. His own charity was profuse, but not without discretion, and included many works not now left to Bishops, though an Act of Elizabeth still expressly recognises them as charitable, the making of causeways and the building of bridges. Nor was this liberality from the teeth outwards. As his early biographer says : " Remembering what heights he had climbed, what as a layman he had neglected, he did his best to redeem the time. Wherefore, as if changed to another man, he set before himself this rule of life : to be on equal terms with his servants, humble to priests, kind to the people, compassionate to the wretched, bountiful to the needy." His visitations of the Priories of St. Swithun and of Selborne, and the drastic proceedings taken to purge the Hospital of St. Cross of its gross abuses, prove the sincerity and courage of the man, as well as the temper and experience of the statesman.

" The College of Oxford stands first, that of Winton second," says the epitaph engraved on Wykeham's tomb in Winchester Cathedral, where he was laid after his death on the 27th of September 1404. But,

indeed, each was required to complete the
other, and the two ideas seem to have
ripened together in Wykeham's mind.
"Our two Colleges," he says in the
Winchester Statutes, "though situate in
different places, spring from one root, and
issue from one fountain." Winchester,
in the more copious language of the New
College Statutes, is to be "the first principle and germ of our Oxford College, the
watered garden and quickening vineyard
from which the buds are to be passed on, to
ripen into fruit and flowers for the service
of God and His Church." In 1375 he
began to collect scholars in Oxford. In
1376 he had there a society of seventy, with
a Warden at its head, which he was obliged
to disperse when the storms gathered about
him—"And so they all departed in great
sorrow and discomfort, weeping and in
simple cheer." But very early in his epis-
copate he had begun to pay for the schooling
of boys in Winchester; and in 1373 he had
formally arranged with a master for the
teaching of "the poor scholars whom the
said Father keeps and shall keep at his own
expense." As soon as his fortunes bright-
ened again, he proceeded to the purchase of
land in Oxford; and in 1379 was in a position to apply to the young King for a
Charter allowing the foundation of a College *de novo*, which should receive a name
hereafter, and to issue his own Charter of
Foundation. On March 5, 1380, the first

stone was laid, and on April 14, 1386, the Society entered upon formal possession of the buildings. Meanwhile, in 1378, he had taken the preliminary steps for his Winchester foundation. In March 1387 the first stone was laid there, and in 1394 the buildings were occupied. The Statutes of both Colleges were drawn up with extreme care and in much detail by Wykeham himself, the first draft being given to New College in 1390 ; but neither code took final shape till the last year of the life of the author. He died at South Waltham on the 27th of September 1404, and was buried in Winchester Cathedral, in the beautiful Chantry Chapel prepared by himself, and recently renovated and adorned by the piety of Wykehamists.

It has ever been the faith of those who have partaken of Wykeham's bounty, that he was in his lifetime a true specimen of the " good great man." Of his goodness we have abundant proof ; of his simple piety, as a boy, and in extreme old age, of his charitable use of his great wealth, of the larger charity which, in the fierce strife of politics, made him, once and again, a mediator and a reconciler, of the sterner virtues of justice and indignation against abuses. Greatness is perhaps the quality which it would have been most foreign to his nature to claim. He moved among great persons, and in great policies, not unquestioned, but when proved not found

18

wanting ; and left behind him the reputation, not, doubtless, of a successful war
minister, but of one who never set personal
gain or the favour of prince or people above
simple duty, of a constitutional statesman
and a lover of England. Perhaps the
moment of his life most truly great was
when his enemies had for the time triumphed,
and he withdrew to his diocese, not to con-
sider in retreat steps for reasserting his
position, but to throw himself heart and
soul into the details of episcopal administration ; until the Bishops found that they
could not do business without the aid of
his sagacity, and the young King persuaded
him that he was indispensable to the State.
His double foundation was great ; great at
once by its scale, and by the novelty of the
conception ; great in the sense in which
"legislators are poets," bringing into being
that which was not in being before ; as the
work of the founders of the American
Constitution, to take an illustration from
the higher politics, was great. We would
willingly have more—a sermon, a letter,
a speech—to show us the man as he was.
That he had a warm human heart his works
show us, and passages in his statutes which
glow with feeling and almost with poetry,
and the considerate tenderness of such provisions as those which he made for the sick
or infirm members of his foundation. We
could wish, too, that Shakespeare had introduced him into his *Richard II.*, so that we

might have had at least an Elizabethan echo of his fame. He was living at the time of the meeting between Bolingbroke and Norfolk, though not then moving prominently in politics. The spirited figure of the Bishop of Carlisle might be taken as reflecting many features of Wykeham's character; and Blake's " Bishop" in his *Edward II.*, with his praises of commerce and of the arts of peace, would assuredly have had our Founder on his side :—

" O my good Lord, true wisdom drops like honey
    From your tongue, as from a worshipp'd oak."

The motto of the College, "Manners makyth man," in the English and in a Latin form, is said to have been a favourite of the Founder's. Perhaps we may recognise the same somewhat sententious wisdom in the words of the Winchester Statutes (Rub. V.): " Comparisons which are odious" ("Comparationes quæ odiosæ sunt "), introduced into a solemn oath; the words are again employed in the severe letter of rebuke which he had occasion to write to his Oxford College in 1385.

A question has been raised in recent years, very interesting to students of Architecture, and somewhat disconcerting to Wykehamical prepossessions. We are told, and apparently on sound reasoning, that we must not speak of the Founder of the two Colleges as an "Architect"; that his experience in early life had been that of a practical surveyor or controller, and that the skilled element in the work of those days was supplied by the master mason, in this case William Winford, as in that of King's College, Cambridge, a century later, it was supplied by Reginald Ely and others. Doubtless there is a fallacy in applying the words of the modern hierarchy, "Architect," "Builder," "Clerk of the Works," to the professional men of the fourteenth century, whether men in broadcloth or men in fustian. But, whatever may have been the Founder's qualifications for originating, or appreciating, the effects of the Perpendicular style, or for himself laying out the details of such a work as the transformation of Winchester Cathedral, we can never doubt that in a very real sense he "traced the plan." The same constructive brain which projected the minute and manifold organisation of his society's daily life, also carried within itself the details of its orderly and beautiful home; he saw before him, with whatever skilled assistance he knew to be needful, the buildings of which it has been said, by one who spoke from a knowledge literally life-long, that "it has only been by living many years, and passing very many other less perfect buildings, that we have come to feel that we lived among the best."

On the great questions of his day it is not easy to quote definite opinions. A thorough Englishman, and with all his bias on the national side, he was yet observant of all

the customary duties to Rome, where he
had been himself regarded with some
jealousy. As a convinced believer in the
supreme importance of Scripture, a belief
which appears again and again in his statutes,
he desired to give the new opinions a hearing, and himself incurred some odium by
shielding an unpopular Wickliffite ; but he
had no sympathy with the petulance and
extravagance which occasionally marked the
movement, and he drew upon himself a tart
polemic from Wicklif.

Of the Founder's personal appearance
there is little authentic record. It is best
preserved to us by a corbel-bust in the
Audit-room of Winchester College, and by
the recumbent figure on his tomb. The
latter is not that of a tall man, but it is
interesting to observe that his father is
said to have borne the name of Long.

The Arms of the College, two black
chevrons and three red roses on a white
field, appear to have been borne by the
Founder in his lifetime, but the second
chevron is said to have been added when
he became bishop. The chevron was a
device used by builders, and was perhaps
adopted by Wykeham with reference to his
skill in architecture. Winchester College
uses the same arms, for most purposes
combined with the keys and sword of
the See of Winchester.

Wykeham's biographer, Bishop Lowth,
perhaps the most learned and accomplished of

his sons, who has spared no pains over the
details of the Founder's life, and especially
in exposing the idleness of certain attacks

ARMS OF COLLEGE IN THE BURSARY

made on his political career in later times,
thus sums up his character :—

"In a word, as he was in his own time a
general blessing to his country, in which his
bounty was freely imparted to any object
that could come within the reach of his
influence ; so the memory of this great man
merits the universal regard of posterity, as
of one, whose pious and munificent designs
were directed to the general good of man-
kind, and were extended to the latest ages."

23

TOWER & CITY WALL.

CHAPTER III

" Nation blest of the Gods ! thy walls already arise ! "
—VIRGIL.

IT was on the Saturday before Palm Sunday, the 14th of April 1386, that the Society left its temporary halls, and, walking in solemn procession, and singing a litany, took possession of the new home. Six years before, on the 5th of March 1380, the first stone had been laid, in the absence of the Founder, who, in November 1379, had, as we have seen, issued his Charter, reciting his purchases of land, declaring the College to consist of a Warden and seventy Scholars (for the ten Chaplains, three Clerks, and sixteen Choristers were an addition made by him later), and assigning to it the name of ·"Sainte Marie Wynchestre in Oxenford." The site had been gradually acquired by him from various vendors, the City of Oxford, Queen's and Merton Colleges, and others. It was an undesirable quarter, being in fact the City Ditch, under the City Wall, the haunt of thieves and the receptacle of filth ; perhaps abandoned to such uses because it had been

25

used as a burying-ground in the years of
pestilence. A jury empanelled for the
purpose had given their verdict that its
acquisition by Wykeham would be of public
advantage. The College into which they
entered was indeed a new one, not only as
the first example on so grand a scale of the
Perpendicular style, but because its organisation was conceived *de novo*. Of the six
Colleges already existing in Oxford, Merton
most nearly resembled it in the scheme of
its foundation ; but, although its still un-
finished Chapel was, and is, a noble pile,
the courts, however interesting, are of
modest dimensions. Queen's, a nearer
neighbour of New College, was projected
on an ample plan, to which it had been so
far impossible to give effect. The view which
met the eyes of the scholars on entering, was
the same which has met our own, but with a
difference. We must imagine Chapel and
Hall as they are to-day, but the upper storey
removed from the three sides of the Quadrangle ; and so restore the far more stately
proportions of the original design, and
enable the tower over the gateway, and
also the Muniment-Tower, once more to
dominate the habitable buildings. We must
also sweep away all the sash windows, and
substitute mullioned and unglazed openings,
and place doors on the hinges which still
remain at the bottom of the staircases. The
oval plot of turf, a beautiful eighteenth
century addition, must go, and a gate be

placed in the middle gateway. A turret
stair leading up to the Warden's lodgings
must be replaced where the Porter's Lodge
now stands. Lastly, it must be remembered
that the Cloisters and the Bell - Tower,
neither of which is in view from where
we stand, were added later, though in the
Founder's lifetime.

The living-rooms were distributed among
the Seventy, the upper chambers having
each three occupants, the lower, with one
exception, four. In each of the larger
chambers were four studies and four windows. The names by which the several
rooms were known have been preserved by
tradition, as The Vine, The Conduit, The
Baptist's Head, &c. To ensure the harmony,
and the balance of special interests, to which
the Founder attached great importance, the
students in the different faculties were to be
mixed together, and one senior in each room
was to have some responsibility for the
others. Late in the sixteenth century attics
were added ; which, a century later, in
1674, were replaced by a third storey, sash
windows being inserted. It was at the same
time that an oriel window was introduced
into the Warden's lodgings, resembling the
one still to be seen there from the outside of
the College. It is interesting to notice that
at Winchester the windows of the Quadrangle were modernised in 1812, but greater
care was there taken to make them harmonise
with their surroundings.

The present Library, contained in the two stories over the gateway of the eastern side of the Quadrangle, is thoroughly modern in its appearance and arrangements, and is of no great general interest, but it includes special collections, formed by former members of the College, and bequeathed to it ; one such collection of works on medicine is of exceptional completeness. Manuscripts, including some which were the gift of the Founder, are preserved in the Auctarium, a closet off the upper room. Among the printed books is a copy of the first printed copy of Aristotle, unique in its integrity, to which Dean Gaisford has given his testimony in an autograph note. A plan for erecting a new Library near the Bell-Tower to form a return upon the Holywell Buildings formed a part of Sir G. Scott's design, and may at a future time come on for consideration. Meanwhile the admirably central position of the present rooms has much to recommend it in point of convenience.

The Hall, the common dining-room, and also the place of meeting for all the more solemn purposes of College procedure, is a noble room eighty feet by forty and very lofty, though the floor is raised high above the level of the Quadrangle. It has been well used by successive generations. The fine panelling is associated with one of the most honoured names of the College, having been placed there by Archbishop

Warham, when Bursar in the reign of
Henry VIII., and was, perhaps, his gift.
The marble pavement replaced the original
floor in 1722. The open oak roof is of
especial interest, both as the first of the
more modern works of restoration, and also
as a contribution, at least in the first place,
made by the junior members of the College.
The original roof had been, at the end of
the eighteenth century, replaced by a ceiling
at the hands of Wyatt, the architect, who
has much to answer for; he had to please
a generation which preferred comfort to
beauty, perhaps we should rather say, which
had convenient, though perverted, ideas of
the beautiful; we enjoy the comfort and
augment it, and we also try to feel our way
back to a truer standard of taste; and it has
yet to be seen, though the living generation
will hardly see it, how posterity will esteem
our conscientious efforts. However this
may be, the Hall roof was felt to be unworthy of its place. The Junior Common
Room, which was practically an independent
corporation, comprising the Undergraduates
and B.A. Fellows and a few Gentlemen
Commoners, its finances varying between
opulence and destitution, according as the
Steward was an economist like Sydney
Smith, or a scatterer, took the first move.
An offer of a thousand pounds out of its
balance at the time was made to the College,
for the purpose of restoring the Hall roof;
which, after somewhat prolonged negotia-

tions, was accepted. In 1865 the work was carried out under the care of Sir Gilbert Scott, the great oak beams being all provided out of woods belonging to the College. The result is exceedingly rich and impressive, the lantern in the middle, a work of strict restoration, being especially admirable. A similar work, but without the lantern, was carried out at Winchester in 1817, being rendered imperative by decay ; and in this case also the beams came out of the College woods. As so little is known about the roof which Wyatt destroyed at New College, an extract from the report of the architect consulted at Winchester (Mr. Garbett), will be of interest :—

"Upon the survey of such a specimen of ancient carpentering the Reporter begs leave to embrace the opportunity it affords of paying his humble tribute of admiration of the simple elegance displayed in the design of this roof, the scientific principles of its construction, the care with which the materials must have been selected, and the accuracy with which the workmanship was executed. To this combination of excellence he attributes the preservation of the work nearly entire through four centuries, while works of contemporary and of subsequent origin have ceased to exist, and have given place to others by no means so favourable to a comparison of Modern with Ancient Taste and Art."

The outlay, of course, many times ex-

ceeded the gift; but to that gift is due the
first impulse to this fine and indeed imperative
work of reconstruction; which records in
imperishable legend the attitude to the whole
Society of its junior members, an attitude
which has been happily maintained through
all changes in the constitution, although the
Junior Common Room does not now, as it
then did, contain any actual or potential
Fellows.

The windows of the Hall were at the
same time filled with painted glass by
Messrs. Clayton & Bell, a bequest by an
old and respected Fellow, who had lately
died, being applied to this purpose. The
portraits, which had before been placed on
the wainscoting, were removed to a higher
level, with the exception of those over the
daïs. Besides that of the Founder, a con-
ventional likeness, may be noticed those of
Archbishop Warham (a copy of a fine
Holbein at Lambeth), of Bishops Ken and
Turner, of Sydney Smith, a refined and
delicate face, and of Sir William Erle,
formerly Chief Justice of the Common
Pleas. Of more strictly contemporary interest are those of the late Warden Sewell,
whose long reign covered the whole period
of the reorganisation of the College, of Mr.
Alfred Robinson, who was associated with
all except its earliest years, and whose special
memorial we shall meet later on, and of
Professor Sylvester of St. John's College,
Cambridge, a Mathematician of the highest

order, who as Savilian Professor of Geometry was for many years before his death a Fellow of New College.

A pleasant association with the old life of the Society may be found in the provisions of the Founder as to the use of the Hall. While he forbids wrestling, dancing, and all noisy games, in the interests both of the adjoining Chapel with its ornaments, and of those who were lodged in chambers below, and enjoins the reading of the Gospel during meals, and the use of Latin in conversation (unless politeness to lay strangers or some other " rational cause " require "another idiom "), he allows a fire to be lighted on high days, when the Fellows and Scholars may linger around it for songs and other honest amusements, and, in a more serious spirit, listen to poems, chronicles of the realms, the natural wonders of the world, and other things befitting the clerical estate. The *Canterbury Tales* were hardly in time to have been read by Wykeham's earliest scholars, and Langland might not have been acceptable ; but there was Laurence Minot, and there was the anonymous *Mort Arthur* and *Sir Gawayne and the Green Knight ;* soon there would be Chaucer and Gower, and, a little later on, Sir Thomas Mallory. Did they read of the wonders of Nature in Sir John Mandeville, who in 1356 had announced that the earth is round, and who had himself discovered Adam's apple, the fruit of which has a bite

taken out of each side? And did a discussion follow?

We descend the stairs again, and pass
under the Hall and Chapel windows, to the
entrance of the latter, noticing by the way
an old carving of the figure of an angel, said
once to have borne in Latin the words,
" This is the Gate of Heaven." The noble
proportions of the Ante-Chapel, used in old
times for lectures and disputations, and still
placed under the eye of the Warden by
means of a window pierced in the wall of
his lodgings, and those of the Chapel itself,
cannot fail to impress eye and imagination.
The ornamental features of the building
have suffered sadly from time and zeal,
partly at the hands of the Reformers, and
perhaps even more under Wyatt. Forty
years ago, it presented a roof of stucco
vaulting, miserably unworthy of its place,
an east end with shallow niches in wood
and plaster, and panelling and carving of
which a large part was plaster, though
details of the old oak work were inter-
mingled or concealed. The organ case
contained a square or oblong opening,
through which the great west window
could be viewed from the body of the
building.

In the Proceedings of the Archæological
Institute, which met at Winchester in 1845,
Mr. C. R. Cockerell wrote :—

" Judging from the copy of Wykeham's
Chapel (*i.e.* that of New College) still

existing in All Souls, it may be presumed that the ceiling and roof were constructed on the hammer-beam system, and not after that more beautiful and expensive manner adopted at Winchester, the reason for which inferiority it would be difficult to discover ; and this opinion is confirmed by the recollection of the venerable survivors of the period of its last repairs. . . . The ceiling is contrary to the geometrical and structural principles of the style, and without model or authority."

As a reconstruction on the lines of the Winchester roof would have been practically impossible, two courses were open to the College. The plan adopted in the case of the Hall might have been followed, and a tie-beam roof erected ; but this would apparently have been a departure from the original lines of the building ; and, further, oak timbers of the required size were not easily to be procured. Following, therefore, the model of the best Perpendicular Churches, especially some fine examples in Norfolk and Suffolk, Sir G. Scott prepared a plan for a hammer-beam roof, reducing the necessary pitch of the roof to the lowest consistent with safety ; and this, after much consideration, was adopted. The drawback is that the roofs of the Chapel and Hall are no longer uniform and continuous. Such interference with the Founder's design as was necessary upon either course appeared to be minimised ; and, considering the great

freedom with which he had himself trans-
formed the old nave of Winchester Cathedral,
the liberty did not seem to be excessive. It
was perhaps not realised till afterwards that
the breach of continuity in the skyline of
the roof would be apparent from so many
points as in fact it is. It must be remembered
that although some of the building in Holywell Street was then standing, this had
hardly come to be thought of as an integral
part of the College. All which we may
hope that posterity will take into account,
when it passes its judgment on those who
added to the interior what in itself appears
to be a dignified and suitable covering.

Of the great beauty and propriety of the
wood-work throughout the Chapel, restored
and continued by Messrs. Farmer and
Brindley in 1879 in harmony with the
ancient misericords and other remains of the
original carving, no question is likely to
arise. The niches of the reredos were provided by Sir Gilbert Scott, and have more
recently been fitted with statues under Mr.
Pearson's superintendence, the general order
being that suggested by the clauses of the
Te Deum.

The present Organ, by Willis, was constructed in 1874, and the case was more
recently adapted to the other woodwork
of the Chapel. Parts of the older instru-
ments by Green (1776) and J. C. Bishop,
also some of that by Dallam (1663), are
included. The original organ was given

by William Porte (1420–3); a poem in
Musæ Hospitales (see p. 57) mentions with
special pride the organ of that date (1610).

The great Perpendicular windows were
specially designed for the exhibition of
painted glass, a growing art in the fourteenth century. The original glass has long
since been removed from the body of the
Chapel, the windows on the south side now
containing the work of foreign artists,
traditionally Flemish, adapted and completed by William Price in 1740; those
on the north, which are greatly inferior,
were filled in only a few years later, in
1768. Some of the tracery lights on both
sides are, however, original. The windows
of the Ante-Chapel are of great beauty and
interest, and have lately been carefully
cleaned, and the proper sequence, which had
been disturbed in a former cleaning, restored, by Messrs. James Powell & Son.
The two eastern windows, originally placed
over altars, contained in their lower lights
representations of the Crucifixion and of
the Twelve Apostles four times repeated ;
the upper lights showed, as did those of the
other windows, various Saints and characters
of the Old and New Testament and of
Church history. But the greater part of
the glass which now fills them is a collection
of fragments without arrangement, the remains of what once filled the windows of
Chapel and Ante-Chapel ; even so pre-
senting, in the lustre and harmony of their

colouring, a beautiful example of fourteenth century art. The great east window of Winchester College contains a likeness of "Thomas the Glazier," and as the name appears among the earliest records as a frequent guest in the Hall of New College, it may be assumed that his hand was at work here also.

We have not yet spoken of the Great West window, which exhibits the famous design of Sir Joshua Reynolds, burnt into glass, but completed by the brush. Of the beauty of the individual lights no one who has seen the groups and figures worked up as easel pictures can doubt; whether they are suitable for the decoration of the building in which they stand is another question. Modern opinion will hardly endorse the greeting of a contemporary poet (T. Warton) :—

> " Thy powerful hand has broke the Gothic charm,
> And brought my bosom back to truth again."

Yet the happily conceived figures of the Virtues, and the fine group of the Shepherds, have given pleasure to very many generations, and it is sad to think that Time is on the side of the more severe critics. It was said that "Sir Joshua had come off with flying colours," and of late years the decay has been rapid, the effect of damp and wind. It has been for the present arrested by enclosing the work within two casings of white glass, recommended and carried out

37

by Mr. Powell. To give scope to the
artist in treating the central group of the
Nativity, where a Rembrandt-like light falls
upon the face of the Infant, the College had
unfortunately consented to remove some of
the tracery. Here Time was more prompt
with his revenge; for it was remembered
that one Sunday, while the Society was at
dinner, a storm of wind and rain drove the
window in, and the missing supports were
afterwards replaced.

The Ante-Chapel contains many interesting and beautiful brasses, the remains
of a number once larger. Those of Thomas
Cranley, 1417, the third Warden, afterwards
Archbishop of Dublin (a fine specimen of
an archbishop in mass-vestments); Richard
Malford, 1403, Warden (represented in pro-
cessional vestments, a cassock, a surplice
covering the feet, almuce, and cope); William
Hautryve, 1441, Fellow (in a rochet or gown
covering the feet, with one small slit in the
hands, through which both hands pass);
John Rede, 1521, Warden (a priest in pro-
cessional vestments); John Gorry, Warden
and Bishop of Callipolis in 1526 (in episcopal
mass-vestments; no year of death); and
Hugh Lloyd of Caernarvon, 1601 (once
Headmaster of Winchester and a fine
Scholar), deserve especial notice. The
brasses are fully described in the *Journal of
the Oxford University Brassrubbing Society*,
vol. i. pp. 41–67.

Near the east end of the Chapel itself is

preserved the Founder's Crosier, a special bequest to New College, and its most treasured relic. It is overlaid with rich tabernacle work of silver gilt and enamel, and resembles a pastoral staff, of work almost equally skilful and artistic, preserved in the treasury of the Cathedral of Cologne. "The form of these pastoral staves is wholly symbolical, the crooked head indicating the pastoral office, the gathering the faithful together. The centre is the emblem of royal power; the sharp point the weapon of judgment." The Crosier was exhibited at South Kensington in 1862. See the *Catalogue*, quoted in R. and R., p. 236, also Mr. Moffat's recent work on Oxford Plate.

The Cloisters and the solid Bell-Tower were a somewhat later addition to the buildings, having been completed

39

and consecrated in 1400. The ribbed roof of
the Cloister is curious and effective. Many
memorial tablets will be found on the
walls (burials within the precincts being
now of very rare occurrence), not the
least beautiful of them being one which
records the services to their country of
the nine members of the College who
fell in the recent South African War
(1899–1902), designed by an Associate of
the Royal Academy, one of many distinguished persons who have received education in the Choir School of the College.

To illustrate the transitory nature of
opinion on æsthetic points, we may quote
one of some "proposals for beautifying
Oxford" printed in 1773 :—

"The West end of the Chapel at New
College, with its stained windows, would
command much attention were it not so
inauspiciously concealed by an antiquated
cloister; if this was away, it would be a
magnificent object."

We return from the Chapel, and passing
the Middle Gateway, find ourselves in the
Garden Quadrangle, built, it used to be said,
after the model of the Palace of Versailles.
The handsome iron screen between it and
the Garden was supposed to have been
brought from Canons, a house of the Dukes
of Chandos, immortalised by Pope as
"Timon's Villa"; a contemporary account,
however, mentions the maker ("that in-
genious Artist, Mr. Thos. Robinson, at

Hyde Park Corner ") and the date (1711). Possibly the legend and the fact may be, in part at least, reconciled. The Garden itself, and its reaches of turf, its vistas showing the finest buildings of Oxford grouped before the eye (of which the view of Magdalen Tower from the left-hand corner at entrance,

THE CORNER BASTION

and that of St. Peter's in the East with its venerable Norman west front, and the conical roofs of two turrets at the eastern angles, should on no account be missed), and more than all, perhaps, the Old City Wall, with its embrasures, now well clothed with foliage, and convenient for the most peaceful pur-

41

poses, hold a high place in the affection of all members of the Society. The art of the gardener, a later, and as Bacon tells us, a more exalted one than that of stately building, seems especially congenial to College residents ; and perhaps there has never been a generation which did not possess a Warden or some Fellow with a happy turn for the conservation and arrangement of trees and flowers. That the feeling is shared by the junior members, we have a touching proof in a young cedar, the gift of a Commoner of the College, who fell in action at Diamond Hill, near Pretoria, on June 12, 1900, and who was found to have made a will, being just of legal age, containing a bequest to the College to be laid out on some purpose connected with the Garden. The lower stretch of lawn was the Bowling Green, but in more recent times was devoted to Archery, now a lost art, which was in great vogue here until the seventies.

The " Mound," which, with its beautiful foliage, relieves the effect to the eye, and breaks the monotony of the turf, was gradually reared and arranged in the course of the sixteenth century. It is thus described in a *Pocket Companion for Oxford* of 1761 :—

" In the middle of the Garden is a beautiful Mount with an easy ascent to the top of it, and the Walks round about it, as well as the Summit of it, guarded with Yew Hedges. The Area before the Mount being divided into four Quarters, in one is the King's Arms, with the Garter and Motto ; in that opposite to it the Founder's ; in the third, a Sun Dial ; and the Fourth, a Garden-Knot, all planted in Box, and neatly cut.

"The whole is surrounded by a Terras. On each side are Lime-trees planted ; and on the North Side in particular there is a *Serpentine Walk* planted with *flowering Shrubs*. Behind the Mount likewise is a fine collection of Shrubs so contrived as to rise gradually one above the other, and over them, a Row of Horse Chestnut Trees, which spread in such a manner as to cover the Garden Wall, and carry the Eye on to a most beautiful Mantle of tall Elms, which terminates the View, and seems to be the only Boundary to that End of the Garden ; but we are obliged to Magdalen College Green for this additional Beauty."

The successors of the chestnuts and of the elms are still with us.

A side gate and walk take us from the garden to the new Holywell buildings. To the left is a fine view of the old City Wall, with the Bell-Tower and the "Slype," a narrow plot of land outside the wall. Of the buildings themselves we have sufficiently spoken. But we must pause for more than a moment before the central gate-tower, designed by Mr. Basil Champneys to connect the older and loftier part of the line with the continuation, on a lower level, to the east. It is the memorial of one whose name will fill a large place in any future record of the College history, as it lives, and will always live, in the hearts of those who were his colleagues or his pupils. Mr. Alfred Robinson, whose figure is shown in a very good likeness on the interior of the tower, became a Fellow of the College in 1865, being a Scholar of University College, and possessing, even then, an extraordinary reputation, earned at Marlborough and in Oxford, not only for the highest academical honours, but for practical wisdom and devotedness in serving his generation. It is always right to remember that the early reforms in New College had proceeded from within. Before the Oxford Act of 1854 the College, with the sanction of the Visitor, had taken the first steps by beginning to admit Commoners, and by allowing the Scholarships at Winchester to be thrown open to competition, an act involving at the time much self-sacrifice. The modifications of the Statutes, contained in the Ordinance of the Commissioners under that Act, were faithfully worked from within ; the motive and directing power being supplied by men, of whom some at least are, happily, with us still. Before 1865, the lines upon which the development was to take place had been securely laid. But much remained to be done, and the period of adolescence was a critical one. Loyally as many of the Fellows most devoted to the old order supported those who were actively fostering the new, there was, as there must be in such a transition, an element of reaction, an atmosphere of suspicion occasionally to be felt. And in the younger part of the Society, too, there was some of the awkwardness of growth,

HOLYWELL BUILDINGS AND ROBINSON TOWER
FROM THE CHAPEL ROOF

the inclusion of new, and, as would now and then happen, of imperfectly assorted materials, the difficulties caused by rapid increase in numbers; even the easy and familiar relations natural in the preceding

45

times between undergraduates, who were themselves Fellows, and their seniors, was capable of being an embarrassment. It was to such a society that Alfred Robinson devoted all the great energies of his mind and heart. With a grave humour which seldom failed to solve any personal difficulties, an iron firmness wherever such a quality was needed, infinite patience for all ordinary follies or crudeness, sympathy alike for the successes of the strong and the helplessness of the comparatively weak, and an instinct which led him to throw his power into any part of the machine which for the moment seemed to flag, his strong personality held all together till the anxious years were safely over. And in the time which followed, in some sense no less anxious, of assured and increasing prosperity, his sane, cautious, statesmanlike foresight, coupled with the warmest of hearts towards individuals and all common interests, made life within the College walls unanimous and peaceful. Greatly valued as a lecturer, and capable of a very high place in the more mature Oxford studies, he took College and University finance for his special field of work, bringing to it the business traditions of a family belonging to the great city of Liverpool, and other gifts of a yet higher order. His health was much broken in his later years, but his work was never interrupted ; it was fulfilled up to nearly the last day of his life ; and he deserves the great praise of leaving to his successors a

46

task rendered easier and not harder to carry on when he was withdrawn. He died young, as we count years, but it might be said with thankfulness of him, as it was written of the Founder, that he completed his task—*Opus feliciter consummavit.*

A gateway forms a very apt memorial to one who had so constantly passed in and out, a part of the general stream of College life. Not less closely associated with the Front Gateway of the College was the venerable form of Warden Sewell ; a very different man from Mr. Robinson, but equally gifted with a single-hearted devotion to the College, a warm affection for every member of it, and a spirit of unswerving rectitude and fairness. He had become a scholar of Winchester in 1821, and had been to the end of his life of full ninety-two years an inmate of one or other of Wykeham's Colleges. His Warden-ship of New College extended over nearly forty-four years, a period very eventful in its history. Himself a Liberal in Academical questions, he had his affections and interests deeply rooted in the past. Changes affecting the life prescribed in the Statutes, or by tradi-tion, always caused him a pang ; but, whether he approved or questioned their usefulness, he accepted them, when once settled, heartily and without any reserve. His skilled hand, which was never idle, may be seen in the antiquarian work of the Library and of the documents of the Muniment-Room, and in many other directions. In the earlier

47

years of his Wardenship, his temper was
cautious and reserved towards individuals,
recalling more nearly the caustic sagacity
of Warden Shuttleworth than the somewhat awe-inspiring grandeur of that fine
scholar and warm-hearted gentleman, Warden David Williams, his immediate predecessor. It became much more genial
as he found that his just and dignified
presidency was so acceptable to others,
more particularly after a singularly successful tenure of the laborious office of
Vice-Chancellor. His service to the College was continued, though at the last with
failing powers, to the very end of his long
life, and is remembered with deep respect
and warm affection. He lies in the north-
eastern corner of the Ambulatory of the
Cloisters, and a tablet in his memory, as also
one to Mr. Robinson, will be found in the
Ante-Chapel.

Tower &
Cloisters

CHAPTER IV

THE UNIVERSITY AND OTHER COLLEGES

" And thou, great Term-time of Oxford,
  Awful with lectures and books, and Little-goes and
  Great-goes!"   —CLOUGH.

WE may be sure that it was not without
anxious thought that Wykeham decided to place his principal College in Oxford, and to make it an integral part of the
University. His first care had been for the
schoolboys of the city where he had himself
been bred. But, as his purpose ripened, and
enlarged itself to meet the needs of Church
and Nation, now grievously weakened by
the years of pestilence, it seemed obvious to
choose one of the Universities ; and, though
Cambridge remembers him as a benefactor,
Oxford was his natural choice, lying nearer
to Winchester, and within the diocese of
Lincoln. As we have seen, he collected
and maintained a body of scholars there, as
early as 1375. We have to think of the
University as a body of some two thousand
clerks, or scholars, lodged, some in religious houses, some in licensed halls,
some in private chambers, of school-
boy age, rough in manners, not springing

from the most refined sections of society, constantly brawling, often with deadly vehemence, amongst themselves, or against the citizens. Into this unorganised mass Colleges, now six in number, had been introduced with a view to providing a common life, not monastic, but orderly and decent, for students of the better sort. The clerk in Chaucer is ready to say a Mass for him that gave him "wherewithal to scolay," and the boon of admission into a College must have won even greater gratitude. The Statutes of Queen's betray an uncertainty as to the University being permanently fixed in Oxford; on the other hand, Merton, by the fact of its foundation, and by the dignity of its buildings, must have gone far to reassure Wykeham on this head.

It was a turbulent neighbourhood into which his scholars were introduced. Less than thirty years had elapsed since the great battle between town and gown of St. Scholastica's day, February 10, 1354, itself the renewal of an older feud. Bells were rung to gather the belligerents on either side : "Slay, slay!" "Havock, havock!" "Smit fast! give good nocks!" were the cries; forty scholars are said to have been killed, and even the scalping of certain clerks is recorded. The site chosen by Wykeham had been, as we have seen, the haunt of "malefactors, murderers, and thieves," and, in all senses of the word,

a nuisance. The official relations with the
City were settled by the Royal Licence of
1379 : the College was to keep the Wall in
repair within its precincts ; and the Mayor
and Burgesses were to have access once in
three years to see that this provision was
carried out, and also for purposes of defence
in war-time. The College Statutes further
provide for a quarterly visitation of the
Wall by the Warden and certain officers, to
be made with great deliberation, and for
the prompt carrying out of necessary repairs.
But these arrangements could not safeguard
individual gownsmen, and it was not without reason that the outer gate was to be
closed at sunset, the other gates at an
earlier hour.

The relations with the University involve
a curious point of academic history, the
exemption of Fellows of New College from
the University Examinations, as we now
call them. It will be understood that the
University was in being before any Colleges,
and that the several Founders of Colleges
placed their houses within its precincts,
in order to ensure for a select number of inmates the advantages of a common and well-
ordered life. In ordinary course, the Student
would present himself for Responsions
after a year of preliminary exercises, and,
after attending lectures in a wider course
of studies, would become a "bachelor";
after some eight years he would take his
M.A. degree, and proceed to "Inception,"

and be installed as a teacher. Wykeham, who provided in his Statutes that ten of his scholars should study Canon, and ten Civil Law, and should proceed to degrees in those Faculties, and that, of those graduating in Arts, two should study Medicine, proceeded to order that the time required by the University should not be accelerated for any of his scholars by "supplication," and that a College Board should inquire into the proficiency of each candidate. The terms of the arrangement, if any, made between the Founder and the University are not known, and it has been conjectured by the learned historian of the Universities of Europe, Dr. H. Rashdall, that the original prohibition passed into a privilege. Certainly, from very early times down to 1834, the privilege existed, and New College men "did not go into the Schools." In 1607 the question was raised by the University, and argued before Archbishop Bancroft as Chancellor; it was then decided in favour of the College. It is understood that Warden Shuttleworth met some resistance offered to the abandonment of the exemption, by making the College examinations prohibitively severe. When the new Honour Schools were set up, at the beginning of the nineteenth century, promising Winchester scholars chafed against what was in fact a check on their reasonable ambition. And there was no reciprocity, since Fellows of New College acted as University Exam-

iners. When, in 1820, it was announced
that Augustus Hare of New College had
plucked Cicero Rabbitts of Magdalen Hall,
the gaiety of Oxford was sensibly increased ;
but it may well have troubled the chivalrous
mind of the victor in that unequal contest
that no academical predecessor in the line
of Rabbitts could ever have sate in judge-
ment on that particular Hare. The similar
exemption in favour of Members of King's
College, Cambridge, the origin of which is
wrapt in even deeper mystery, was only re-
nounced in 1852, though it had long been felt
to be an incumbrance. Certainly, neither
College has had reason to complain of the
results which have followed the renunciation.

In the offices which most easily mark
the contribution of a College to the common
life of the University, New College can
show a distinguished record. Thus in the
eighteenth century there were three Professors of Poetry—Joseph Spence, Robert
Lowth, and Robert Holmes ; as the usual
term of office was then ten years, the
number alone is remarkable, but all are
names of mark, though in different degree.
There was also a Public Orator, William
Crowe. The first Librarian appointed by Sir
Thomas Bodley in 1598 was Thomas James,
an indefatigable and competent scholar ; and
the office was filled for nearly half of the
nineteenth century by Dr. Bandinel. There
were many Professors of Greek, of Hebrew,
and of other subjects.

Such academical distinctions as were open to undergraduates fell with very fair frequency to New College. The Latin Verse Prize came to it seven times in the early or middle nineteenth century, and six times in the eighteenth. A still more in-

ST. PETER'S CHURCH FROM THE GARDEN

teresting witness survives in a little volume called *Peplus*, edited by John Lloyd, of Denbigh, afterwards Regius Professor of Greek, being a collection of Latin poems written on the occasion of Sir Philip Sidney's death in the preceding year (1586),

56

most of them made "by New Coll.
Scollers." The Latinity and versification
appear to be excellent ; which was to be
expected from the high standard attained
at Winchester, as shown by the addresses
made to Edward VI. in 1552 (Leach's
History of Winchester College, p. 281).
What is further worthy of note, in view
of the charge which came to be current
later, perhaps not undeservedly, that New
College produced " Golden Scholars, Silver
Bachelors, Leaden Masters, Wooden Doc-
tors," is that no fewer than five of the
contributors to *Peplus*, all New College
scholars, have a place in the *Dictionary of
National Biography*. In 1610 a somewhat
similar volume, in equally good Latin, *Musæ
Hospitales Wiccamicæ*, was compiled on the
occasion of the visit of the Duke of Bruns-
wick.

Even closer than its relations with the
University were those between New
College and Winchester, for these were
of the essence of the Founder's scheme.
We have already quoted from the Statutes
of both Colleges for the intended spirit of
the connection : the particular provisions
are precise. In the first place, all the
scholars of New College were to be drawn
from Winchester, a preference being given
to those of kin to the Founder. There
were seventy in each body, and the succession was of course much more rapid in
the School than in the Oxford College, so

57

that the greater number of the Winchester
scholars had to look elsewhere for a home.
As the system came to be worked, the
order was settled in the middle part of
the school; after that it was a mere question of rotation. Many are the stories of
bitter disappointment, not always in the
long run a misfortune to the sufferer,
summed up in the words, " No vacancy";
and many the instances of excellent scholars
whose way was blocked by a " Founder,"
the member of one of the families whom
Wykehamists agreed to respect, but whose
actual " consanguinity" may have been or
the thinnest.

The second point was that the Warden
of Winchester was appointed by New
College; the ten priest-fellows of Winchester being to some extent an after-
thought, and corresponding rather to the
ten chaplains of New College than to the
Fellows. The intention is very clear that
the Warden of New College should be the
higher both in dignity and in emoluments.
Unfortunately all the Wardens of Winchester had not displayed the strong character
and ready munificence of a Harris in the
seventeenth century, or the noble simple-
mindedness of a Barter in the nineteenth;
and, in spite of repeated remonstrances from
Visitors, the Winchester Office became the
richer of the two. Seven Wardens of New
College in succession, covering a period
little short of a century, sought and obtained

promotion by becoming Wardens of Winchester. This perversion of the Founder's intention was at last brought to an end by the Visitor, who declared the Warden of New College of the day to be ineligible. The decision was based on highly technical, it might almost seem, sophistical reasoning; but the practical objection urged by Lowth and others, in a controversy which followed, against continuing the practice of the last six elections, was that undergraduate Fellows, who, in point or discipline, were subject to the Warden, ought not to be called upon to vote on a question of his preferment. The office is now much modified, and the appointment has been transferred to the Fellows of Winchester.

A third provision of great importance was the Visitorial power given to New College, and usually exercised in the Scrutiny held at the time of the Annual Election at Winchester, the three New College Electors (the Warden and the two "Posers") sitting for this purpose without their Winchester Colleagues, hearing complaints, and instituting inquiries. Though the Bishop of Winchester claimed, and was allowed to have, as the Ordinary for the time being, a concurrent authority, it is only by recent legislation that he has become the Visitor, the powers of New College having passed away with the old ceremonies of the Election.

59

Wykeham solemnly charged his two Colleges mutually to support one another in all suits and controversies; and the spirit of his injunction that they should present a united front to the world outside has never been allowed to become obsolete.

This community of interests between New College and Winchester is further recognised in the oath to be taken by individual scholars of the former upon admission to Fellowship, in which they undertook to observe the statutes and protect the prosperity of both Colleges, and to reveal no secrets which might come to their knowledge to the prejudice of either.

A development of this principle of mutual protection, which is of great historical and sentimental interest, is the famous "Amicabilis Concordia," an agreement entered into in 1464 by the Wardens and Provosts of the two double foundations of New College and Winchester, King's College (then called St. Mary and St. Nicholas) in Cambridge, and Eton, wherein each recognises a community of purpose with the other, and undertakes to support and defend it in all causes wherein either may be involved.

The times which followed were dangerous to new foundations; Eton narrowly escaped extinction at the hands of Edward IV., and Winchester at those of Henry VIII.; and it may well be that a generous recognition of this duty of mutual help served both bodies in good stead. But at least one express appeal to the "Amicabilis Concordia" made in much later times is on record. In April 1702, shortly after Queen Anne's accession, Warden Traffles of New College went to London to obtain the withdrawal of a Letter granted by the late King to request the election of one Will. Egerton to a scholarship. He wrote in his journal :—

"Ap. 10.—I called on the Provost of Eaton to engage him to assist ye Coll : in this matter by the interest of his brother ye Ld. Godolphin. I delivered a copy of ye agreement between King's, Eaton, New, and Winton Colleges. He told me that he had already a copy of it, assured me of his hearty assistance, and that all honest men would help it forward."

It is satisfactory to know that William III. had already received a petition on the subject, to which he had graciously replied that "God forbid that he sho'd hinder any of his Colleges from observing their Statutes"; also that Will. Egerton was elected to a scholarship, in ordinary course, in the following year.—*Kirby's Annals*, pp. 523–5.

If this Agreement is now matter for the antiquarian, the original foundation of the two Colleges of Henry VI. is a great and vital fact in the history of those of Wykeham. The idea of a school feeding a College in the University was borrowed

by the King from the Bishop; the first
six Eton scholars were drawn from Winchester; and Waynflete, who was at the
time Headmaster of Winchester, became
first Headmaster, then Provost, of Eton,
and, later on, Bishop of Winchester. It was
he who, as Provost, signed the "Amicabilis
Concordia" for Eton. In quite modern
times, it has happened to New College to
draw many of its foundation members, and
a large proportion of its whole numbers,
from Eton; and it is pleasant to recognise
that the connection, which is so strong in
the present, rests on a sure foundation of
history.

The mention of William Waynflete re-
minds us of his own beautiful College of
St. Mary Magdalen, between which and
New College there is an historical tie;
not only because it was founded, as was
Corpus Christi College, the home of many
eminent Wykehamists, by a successor of
Wykeham in the See of Winchester, but
also because Waynflete made the Fellows
of New College eligible for the office of
President. Indeed, if tradition speaks true
here, though no direct evidence can be
quoted, he was ready to devote his great
wealth to the augmentation of Wykeham's
foundation, had not the Fellows of New
College preferred to retain an undivided
debt of gratitude to their "Sole and munificent Founder."

Lastly, the Statesman-Prelate Chichele,

who had been educated by Wykeham, and had afterwards been a Fellow of New College, followed his benefactor's plan in designing All Souls, the foundation of his old age, especially in the arrangement of the Ante-Chapel, Chapel, and Hall, and in adopting the Perpendicular architecture throughout.

In recent years All Souls has increased its obligation to Wykeham, and at the same time in some sense acquitted it, by adopting as Fellows not a few scholars and commoners of the older foundation.

CHAPTER V

THE HISTORY OF FIVE HUNDRED YEARS

> "Be it so!
> Enough if something from our hands have power
> To live, and act, and serve the future hour."
> —WORDSWORTH.

WHEN William of Wykeham died, in 1404, his two colleges were launched, each upon its independent course, over the troublesome waters which lay before them ; to be steered, so far as might be in concert, according to the two bodies of Statutes, which became irrevocable by his death. He was not so unversed in human nature as to suppose that all possibility of corruption could be eliminated by a Code. Even in 1385 he had been moved to write a severe rebuke, accompanied by notice of a personal visitation, to his Oxford College, a vineyard in which the wild grapes of jealousy and irregular living were already taking the place of lawful fruit. To a courtier, who had taunted him with establishing a school of Lollardism, he had replied : "God forbid that I should expect that my little hostel should be happier than the ark of Noah, which carried a reprobate ; or than the house of Abraham, which contained an Ishmael."

64

For some four hundred and fifty years, while England was passing from era to era, whether under stress of revolution in Church and State, or in unmarked growth during

THE COLLEGE FROM THE GARDEN

long intervals of tranquillity, perhaps of drowsiness, the College life was governed absolutely by the Founder's scheme. The additions to the original fabric mark successive stages in the growing standard of decency and comfort outside, but any constitutional development was precluded ; and we can name few innovations which even savour of organic change before the passing of the Act of 1854, and the framing of an Ordinance in 1857, which superseded in

65   E

most points the Founder's Provisions, and was itself superseded by Statutes made under the Act of 1877. Such an innovation was the presence of a married Warden. The Founder had not made matrimony a cause for the removal of the Warden, as he had in the case of the Fellows; and the office, being a clerical one, followed the general law; this change dates from the early sixteenth century. Again, the preference to be given to the Founder's kinsmen, which had almost fallen into abeyance, was revived late in the sixteenth century, on the claim of a member of a particular family, since intimately and honourably connected with both Colleges. The claim had been disallowed by the Visitor, but the Lord Keeper of the day took it upon himself to reverse his decision. The preference was afterwards regulated by the orders of various Visitors, and, in the state of things which preceded its abolition, two " Founders " used to be elected into each College every year. The occasional admission of Gentlemen Commoners, which in the case of New College was an irregularity (at Winchester a small class of non-foundation pupils had been permitted by the Founder), need hardly be considered here, though some of the most distinguished alumni of the College were non-foundation members. The gradual relaxation of the clerical restriction, in literal accordance with the Statutes, though not intended to be general, led to the result that, although the majority of the Fellows at any one time were in fact in Holy Orders, no single Fellowship could be described as clerical. The practice of general permissive non-residence of Fellows appears to date from the seventeenth century.

It remains to notice some incidents in the history of the College, and some members who were prominent in it, or who have left a name interesting to the larger public, as well as to partial students of its annals.

In its early years New College produced an abundant crop of scholars such as the Founder had desired ; men well grounded in sound elements of " grammar," prudent in affairs, and skilful lawyers, untouched, perhaps, for the most part, by disturbing enthusiasm in things intellectual or religious. In the stirring of the waters which preceded the Reformation, and which is associated with the great English names of Colet, Grocyn, Lynacre, and More, Wykeham's foundations are honourably represented by the second on the list. William Grocyn, the son of a New College tenant at Colerne, in Wiltshire, was a scholar of Winchester from 1463 to 1467, and then a Fellow of New College until 1481, when he became Rector of Newnton Longville, in Buckinghamshire, in the gift of the College ; which has recently done itself honour by placing a brass tablet in the Church to the memory of its first Greek scholar. He was also made a reader of Magdalen College, and in that capacity took part in a disputation held in the presence of King Richard III. and Bishop Waynflete. In 1485 and the following year he travelled in Italy, and attended the lectures of Politian, and other scholars of the day. Returning to Oxford in 1491, he occupied rooms in Exeter College, and lectured daily in Greek. As, however, Greek lectures had been given in New College by one Cornelio Vitelli, under an arrangement made by Warden Chandler, as far back as 1488, it is well to believe that Grocyn learnt his Greek, and perhaps began to teach it, within the walls. His learning was of a more old-fashioned type than that of the contemporary humanists in England; he never dropped the Schoolmen, and greatly preferred Aristotle to Plato, " much science " to " much myth." A single letter, in which this preference is stated, and an epigram addressed to a lady who had thrown a snowball at him, are all that remain of his writings; indeed, partly owing to poor eyesight, he was a sparing writer, though a ready talker and fond of his jest. His library, of which we have a list, included works of Aristotle and of Plutarch, and treatises on Astronomy. He died poor, his plate being at the time in pawn to John Yonge, Master of the Rolls, himself a former Fellow, who by his will directed its free return.

The College Statutes contained a novel provision for the appointment of tutors (" informatores ") to assist younger students; and Grocyn was tutor to one who afterwards held the highest offices, and served with credit in great negotiations of State, William Warham, Archbishop of Canterbury, and Lord High Chancellor, and also Chancellor of the University. Erasmus gives a lively account of a visit to Lambeth, made in company with Grocyn, who introduced the witty foreigner to his illustrious old pupil. Warham left the College his Law library, and his "prick song books." We have already seen proofs of his taste, perhaps also of his munificence, in the Hall. Winchester College owes to him a gift of several fine pieces of tapestry, which were recently exhibited at South Kensington, and have now been placed in the chapel of Winchester, the walls of which they greatly enrich. He ended his days with little more worldly gear than his comparatively obscure tutor; and having asked on his death-bed how much money there was, and being told "thirty pounds," replied, in Latin words: "Enough for the journey-money!"

To a body of students, incorporated under a somewhat narrow rule, the long years, during which the English Reformation was at last effected, must have been a time of intense strain and of searching trial. Questions had to be settled by each individual touching his innermost life, spiritual and intellectual, yet put to him mostly in a gross and concrete form, with a frowning tyrant, or his emissary, awaiting the answer. Small wonder if some gave a hesitating reply, if the stock of the waterman, who looks one way and rows another, was not unrepresented, if a few chose the line of least resistance, and of greatest apparent gain. Small wonder, too, if the bias of the Fellows was on the whole towards the older and more familiar form of faith, so that many, including perhaps the most learned of their number, defied consequences, and ended their days in retirement or prison at home, or in foreign seminaries. Such, to name two out of a much larger number, were John and Nicholas Harpesfield, the latter of whom fled to Louvain in 1556, held high offices under Mary, and finally died in the Tower in 1575. The Protestants had their representatives and even their martyrs; as Peter Quinby, a Lutheran, who in 1533 was imprisoned in the College Tower in the time of Warden London, and died there of starvation and cold; and William Forde, Second Master of Winchester, a Puritan who had the courage of his opinions, and "hadde a dogge lyff" in consequence among his colleagues and scholars.

The years which followed were marked by scholarship of a high order, in both Colleges; and academic life was beginning to settle into something like modern condition, when the Civil War came; an interruption, because arms will always thrust

studies into a corner ; a distraction, because
it made the atmosphere of a Court familiar
to Oxford. New College did not play a
specially prominent part in the struggle ; it
gave its plate, as is now clearly established,

THE CLOISTER WALK

other than the sacred vessels of the Chapel,
to the King ; and the excellent Warden
Pinke, acting Vice-Chancellor, who had
been the first to organise the University
Volunteers, was seized at Aylesbury by
the Parliamentary commanders and sent
to London, to answer for his share in

the defensive works of the City. A thoroughfare was engineered into Queen's Lane. The Tower and Cloisters became an arsenal, and the Choristers' School was removed to the long dark chamber under the Hall, long associated with the proceedings of the old-fashioned Gaudy, and now used in part as a store-room. Antony Wood was a pupil in the School, having been taken away from Thame School in consequence of the troubles, and remembered the exercises of the University Train-bands taking place in the Quadrangle : " And it being a novel matter, there was no holding of the schoolboys in their school in the Cloyster from seeing and following them, and . . . some of them were so besotted with the training and activities and gayities of some young scholars, as being a longing condition to be one of the traine, that they could never be brought to their books again."

After Naseby, and the surrender of the City of Oxford in 1646, the Parliamentary Visitors proceeded to deal with the Colleges, but gradually, and with evident forbearance. It was not till 1649 that Warden Stringer, elected on Pinke's death in defiance of a suspensory order, was ousted, and George Marshall, a graduate of Cambridge, intruded into his place. In August 1651, Colonel Draper, Governor of the City, fortified New College for the Parliament, to the no small injury of the fabric, the cloister being pierced for musketry : " A strong stone tower of defence was built in the centre of the Court ; but Master John Kent, one of the Fellows, rode on the King's side, at the head of one hundred and fifty horsemen, who took the motto ' Non Arte sed Marte.' " On August 25 there was a review of ten companies of the University Volunteer Corps in New College Court.

Again, for the last time, let us hope, under stress of civil troubles, arms were seen and heard in the precincts of the College, when, in 1685, during Monmouth's rebellion, Robert Sewster, Fellow of the College, a M.A. of twenty years' standing, commanded a company of University Volunteers, mostly of New College, and exercised them in the Bowling Green, the lawn at the end of the garden, as it now is. Again in 1798, under the captaincy of John Coker, a former Fellow, and once and again since 1859, the same ground has echoed with a like response to a call which will never be disregarded :—

> " . . . but of kindred birds
> I do forbid the battle."

During the winter of 1665–6, while the plague was raging in London, the Court of Charles II. had been lodged in Oxford. The Spanish Ambassador was entertained in the lodgings of the Warden of New College, and left as a present to the College a large and very handsome cup of silver-gilt, the Grace Cup of the present day. As the older plate, with the exception of some of that belonging to the Chapel, and of some beautiful and interesting pieces in the keeping of the Warden (a fifteenth century salt-cellar, two cocoa-nut cups, &c.), had been given to the Royal cause, the cup remains, next to the Crosier, the principal possession of the College, in its intrinsic and historical value.

The reign of James II. brings before us two names honoured in the record of English liberty, those of Francis Turner, Bishop of Ely, and Thomas Ken, Bishop of Bath and Wells, both Fellows of New College, the former the senior by a year. In a musical society which met weekly at the house of the organist of St. John's, " Thomas Ken, a junior, would be sometimes among them, and sing his part." He was a Fellow of Winchester College from 1666 until he became a Bishop ; and an organ, which stood in his room there, was remembered far into the eighteenth century as " Dr. Ken's organ." He would also accompany himself on his lute. He was brother - in - law of Isaac Walton. His memory carries with it an indescribable fragrance, and we could wish that any record of his life in New College had been preserved to us.

William Somerville, the author of *The Chase*, a hearty sportsman and no mean poet, was a Fellow from 1694 to 1704. It is unfortunate, and in the one case even deplorable, that there was no vacancy for

William Collins or Edward Young; and
that other Winchester poets, as John Phillips
and Joseph Warton, should have passed to
other colleges. A like regret may be ex-
pressed, to go back to an earlier date, for
Sir John Davys, Solicitor-General of Ire-
land at the beginning of James I.'s reign,
author of *Nosce Teipsum*, a metaphysical
poem of very great merit. A tradition in
his family, but we fear a groundless one,
assigns him to New College: he really went
from Winchester to Queen's. A considerable name belonging to a still earlier generation, is that of George Turberville, who
became a Fellow in 1561, and was afterwards Secretary to the Russian Legation, a
poetical stylist of much merit and some
success.

Among the men of the eighteenth century who held important academical offices,
is one whose reputation appeals to a larger
audience. Robert Lowth was the son of a
Prebendary of Winchester, and was a scholar
of Winchester College, passing to New College in 1729, where he resided as a Fellow
until 1750. He was afterwards Bishop suc-
cessively of St. David's, Oxford, and London,
and died in 1787. Wykehamists owe him
a large debt of gratitude for his learned and
judicial Life of their Founder; his stately
lines on the Jesse window of Winchester
College Chapel, written and published, without his knowledge, while he was still at
school, are worthy of their subject. He is

75

more widely known by his original and
eloquent *Lectures on Hebrew Poetry,* delivered from the Chair of Poetry in Oxford,
which "seemed," a competent critic has told
us, "to combine the polish of a past generation with the learning of a new period to
come," and which may still be read with
admiration and pleasure; and by his English
translation of the *Book of Isaiah,* a later
work. The Lectures involved him in a
controversy with Warburton; his *Letter*
to whom has been ranked, as a master-
piece of English style, with Burke's *Speech
to the Electors of Bristol,* Johnson's *Preface
to Shakespeare,* and Parr's *Dedication.* As
there are not too many green resting-places
in the somewhat monotonous expanse of
eighteenth century life in an Oxford College, a few sentences of the *Letter* may be
quoted. They have already been quoted,
though hardly endorsed, by Gibbon, whose
own acquaintance with Oxford was of the
briefest :—

"For, my lord, I was educated in the
University of Oxford; I enjoyed all the
advantages, both public and private, which
that famous seat of learning so largely affords.
I spent many years in that illustrious society,
in a well-regulated course of useful discipline and studies, and in the agreeable
and improving commerce of gentlemen and
scholars; in a society where emulation
without envy, ambition without jealousy,
contention without animosity, incited in-

dustry and awakened genius; where a liberal pursuit of knowledge, and a generous freedom of thought, was raised, encouraged, and put forward by example, by commendation, and by authority. I breathed the same atmosphere that the Hookers, the Chillingworths, and the Lockes had breathed before."

John Wesley spoke with great appreciation of Lowth's Lectures, and it is recorded of Lowth that he refused to sit above John Wesley at dinner.

Before the eighteenth century had run out, it redeemed itself from any reproach of mediocrity by giving New College its most brilliant son in Sydney Smith; who was born in 1771, was a scholar of Winchester 1782–8, a Fellow of New College until his marriage in 1800, and a Canon of St. Paul's from 1832 until his death in 1844. Of his life in College, it is strange to write, no personal reminiscences are forthcoming, nor does he himself refer to it. He quotes, however, the saying of a friend of those days: "Sydney, your sense, wit, and clumsiness always give me the idea of an Athenian carter." One record is significant: Sydney Smith was Steward of the Junior Common Room; a fact which in itself is no small tribute to his capacity, for his means were narrow, and the habits of the day sumptuous. Among the archives of that institution, of which his well-kept accounts form part, is a note in his handwriting, to the effect that coals should be

stored in the summer months, when the
canal rates are low. Here is the future
Treasurer of St. Paul's, of whom Dean
Milman writes : " I find traces of him in
every particular of Chapter affairs ; and on
every occasion where his hand appears, I
find stronger reason for respecting his sound
judgment, knowledge of business, and
activity of mind ; above all, the perfect
fidelity of his stewardship."

All the world knows Sydney Smith as the
most delightful, because the most spon-
taneous and the kindliest, of jesters. But
the noble depth and dignity of speech, and
the indomitable courage, which were his
equally essential gifts, may not always be
equally well remembered. " Why truth
may not be gay I cannot see," said Horace.
But Sydney Smith was not merely a
humorist who sometimes dared to hint a
deeper moral. His Assize sermon on
" The Judge that smites contrary to the
Law," and the sermon " On the Duties
of the Queen," preached at the time of
William IV.'s death, are of the purest
water of pulpit eloquence. A passage on
National Spirit and another on the Love
of Knowledge in his Edinburgh Lectures
are selected by Ruskin as two noble examples of English prose " most impressive,
because steel-true." The *Edinburgh Review*
articles, which form a bulky volume, are
masterpieces of clear thought and lively
expression. But more remarkable than their

78

style is the long list of causes, then forlorn, but long since triumphant, of which he was the champion. "Chimney Sweepers," "Spring Guns," "Counsel for Prisoners," "Catholic Disabilities," are a few of the headings.

Among the abuses at which Sydney Smith tilted was the exclusive honour paid to the classical languages in education. To their intrinsic beauty, and to the reasons for continuing their study within sensible limits, he was keenly alive. "Compared to them," he wrote, "merely as vehicles of thought and passion, all modern languages are dull, ill-contrived, and barbarous." His brother "Bobus" has left us perhaps the most beautiful of all specimens of modern Latin verse-writing, and all the brothers had the gift. If a Common Room discussion on this subject could be arranged between Bishop Lowth and Sydney Smith, both holders of views in advance of their times, and conducted in the perfectly modulated periods of eighteenth century diction on the one side, and the more vivacious, but equally regular sentences of the early Victorian standard on the other. it might help us greatly in some of our modern difficulties.

One reference to a school and College contemporary we are glad to have. Speaking of a measure as to Church patronage, which the new Ecclesiastical Commission was contemplating, Sydney Smith writes :—

"I was at school and college with the

Archbishop of Canterbury ; fifty-three years ago he knocked me down with the chess-board for checkmating him, and now he is attempting to take away my patronage. I believe these are the only two acts of violence he ever committed in his life."

The Archbishop was William Howley, Sydney's Smith's senior as a Fellow by a few years, a learned and amiable prelate, who baptized Queen Victoria, and to whom it fell to announce to her, awakened for the purpose, that she was " The Queen."

A Reformer of a different type, but a man of beautiful mind and character, was Augustus William Hare, who came up from Winchester in 1810. He is best known as the elder brother of Julius Hare, and joint author with him of *Guesses at Truth*, a volume of brilliant notes on literary and speculative subjects, somewhat after the manner of Coleridge ; also as the author of what have been called the best Parish Sermons ever published. He became a tutor, and resided until his marriage in 1829 ; he then settled in the small College living of Alton Barnes, on the edge of Salisbury Plain, which was his home until his early death in 1834. The story of his ministry there, and of his domestic life, one of singular beauty, has been told by his nephew in the *Memorials of a Quiet Life*. His generous and enthusiastic temperament attached him to all his pupils, all the more so because of many peculiarities of manner.

"He was *very* eccentric," was the verdict of those who knew him.

His undergraduate life had been a bright

MAGDALEN COLLEGE TOWER FROM
THE GARDEN

one, spent in "the Garden rooms," which he retained to the end of his residence, "with their view of grey lawns and chestnut trees and Magdalen Tower." The tutors whom he found in College do not seem to have troubled themselves much with tuition ; but this, however reprehensible, may have been a blessing in a sense. He was an original member of the "Attic Society," lately founded on the lines of a Cambridge Club of that day, and taking its name partly from the lofty rooms in which it sometimes met, partly from the Attic salt which seasoned its transactions. It centred in Trinity, and four New College names occur in an early list ; there were also many of Hare's Winchester friends, among them Archdeacon Randall, then at Trinity, and Thomas Arnold, scholar of Corpus. It was after a meeting of the Attic Society that Augustus Hare arranged an excellent hoax, a sham despatch in the true Napoleonic style, announcing a sham victory, that of "Altendorn," by which the University was beguiled for the space of a whole Sunday. A still more elaborate joke, in which no less a person than Madame de Staël is introduced, is told by Hare's biographer from the reminiscences of a contemporary :—

"It was announced that she was in England, and was about to visit Oxford, where she had an undergraduate friend. For a few weeks the undergraduate who was to be so highly honoured became a subject of universal interest. At length it was noised abroad that the great lady had arrived; and under the extraordinary circumstances the undergraduate ventured to invite several of the heads of houses, and even the Vice-Chancellor himself, to meet her at breakfast. The party assembled ; Madame de Staël was there, and so charmed everybody by her grace, wit, and brilliancy, that they all went away feeling that they had found her even more than they anticipated. It was not till many weeks after that it was discovered that she had never been at Oxford at all, and that she had been represented by a clever undergraduate, who had resided for many years in France."

We have called Augustus Hare a reformer, for he struck early and struck hard at two weak points in the constitution of the College. One was the exemption from University examinations, on which he printed a letter while an undergraduate. At the same time he is said to have impugned the preference given to Founder's kin. What is certain is that he raised the point deliberately when acting as " Poser " at Winchester ; and that the question was argued before the Visitor sitting with Assessors, several years afterwards, and decided against the Appellant, who had chosen the ground that by the Canon Law presumption, which was in the Founder's mind, consanguinity was exhausted after the tenth degree. If this was really so, the Founder's denunciations of those who, beguiled by the old serpent, might seek to vary his dispositions, did not apply. Never-

theless, it is not difficult to see that the
author of the proceedings would be looked
on with little approval by the powers of the
College. In after years, Hare was spoken
of as a man who might be chosen for the
Wardenship of Winchester, an office which
was clearly well suited to his ability, and
which he might have greatly adorned, had
it fallen to him.

The Junior Counsel for Hare at this
hearing was a Fellow who bore the Wykehamical name of Erle; afterwards Sir
William Erle, Chief Justice of the Common
Pleas, "a Judge," as he has been described
by a very high legal authority, "very zealous
for justice," a generous, compassionate, liberal
(in every sense of the word), and public-
spirited man. With him, and the Lord
Justice Sir George Giffard, an Equity
Judge of high reputation, and with two
other laymen, we may close this list, the
brothers John and Philip Duncan, whose
portraits we have seen in the Hall, not
public men in the fullest sense of the word,
but admirable specimens of a type, that
of the "rich man furnished with ability,"
large-hearted and open-handed, to which
English society owes so much. We ought
to add, however, that a closer scrutiny of the
various orders within the College since its
foundation, the Chaplains—amongst whom
comes the great name of Isaac Barrow—the
Organists, the Bible Clerks, the Choristers
and pupils of the Choir School, the more

recent body of Choral Scholars, and the
non-foundation members perhaps best ex-
emplified by Sir Henry Wotton, and more
recently by the second Lord Redesdale,
will furnish proof that the College,
however worthily represented, as well as
governed, by the Warden and Fellows,
has not depended upon them exclusively
for its reputation.

CHAPTER VI

THE OLD AND THE NEW

"Joy to the oak of the mountain : he trusts to the
    might of the rock-clefts ;
Deeply he mines, and in peace feeds on the wealth
    of the stone."

—C. KINGSLEY.

IF our last chapter had covered a complete
five hundred years of the College's history it should have ended in 1879, in which
year the five hundredth anniversary of the
Founder's Charter of Foundation was cele-
brated in the presence of the Visitor (Bishop
Harold Browne), and the Chapel reopened
after its renovation. A reference to the
University Calendar of that year would
show a Society not widely different in numbers and arrangement from that of 1906, at
any rate bearing far more resemblance to it
than to what we should find in 1856, the
year in which the last Scholar elected under
the original Statutes came up from Winchester. In that year we should find, as at
any time during the four centuries and a
half preceding it (some years of the Civil
War and Commonwealth excepted), a
Warden, seventy Fellows, of whom some
were undergraduates—a few of them more

86

properly termed Scholars, being in their two years' term of probation—ten Chaplains, three Bible Clerks, and sixteen Choristers, to which number had been added an Organist and a few Gentlemen Commoners. Of the graduate Fellows, about six, holding tutorships and the "Offices," and a very few others, would be resident, the larger number would be elsewhere, holding curacies or the less valuable College livings, or engaged in school work, or at the Bar or other professions. Looking beyond this bare record, we should find that the College held a considerable position in Oxford, certainly not due to its numbers, but rather to its wealth, its antiquity, its spacious buildings, and to the liberal tastes and practical ability of some of its members. Within the walls, we should observe some of the characteristics to be expected in a small society of foundation members, all drawn from the foundation of one school, not a large one, and inheriting traditions which pointed to a life isolated, in many respects, from that of the University at large.

It may not be without interest to those who have followed so far this brief record, if we glance for a moment at the Society of the present day, as it appears in the list contained in the University Calendar of 1906. It shows a Warden, twenty-seven Fellows, and four Honorary Fellows (all former members of the College who have attained special distinctions in Church or State), forty-three Scholars, two Chaplains, an Organist, a Schoolmaster, eight Lay Clerks, and eighteen Choristers. The non-foundation members in residence are some two hundred in number, being Undergraduate or B.A. Commoners. Of the Fellows, five are Professors in the University, three are engaged on scientific or literary work in the University, irrespective of any College obligations; three still hold under the original Statutes, one, originally elected under those Statutes, holds under special provisions of more recent date, and two under the Ordinance of 1857. The administrative and teaching staff consists of a Bursar and ten Tutors or Lecturers, to whom are to be added four Lecturers who belong also to other Colleges. Of the Scholars, about half come from Winchester, six being usually elected in every year, and now drawn from the whole School. Some hundred and thirty undergraduates live within the walls; the rest of the two hundred, being for the most part those who have already passed two or three years in College, in lodgings outside. Among the Commoners are included seven " Rhodes Scholars," and also several students engaged in work of advanced "research," under the special provisions made by the University.

In all forms of athletics the College holds an honourable place in Oxford. Its rowing record necessarily belongs to somewhat modern history, since the numbers in older days were quite insufficient to provide an

Eight. It first attained the first place on the river in 1887, and has occupied it, on and off, in the races of eleven years. In other kinds of activity it is not easy to give tangible facts without going into tedious detail; but in cricket at least we can point to a long list of representatives in the University Eleven, going back to a remote time, when the College was practically drawn from one School. The beautiful ground near the Upper Cherwell, a monument of Mr. Alfred Robinson's enlightened policy in College finance, and a handsome barge on the river, designed and built for the College in 1899, are features in the corporate life of no mean significance.

Prophecy is a dangerous, and usually an idle, pastime, and we will not attempt a forecast of the College, as the future may fashion it. The numbers at least seem to have reached their utmost possible expansion. Its roots are planted firmly in the past; it draws strength from the large conception of William of Wykeham, from the genius of his more gifted sons, and from multitudes of faithful and patriotic lives which have passed unmarked here, but have not passed in vain. In the present, it is nourished by the life of the nation, in every ramification of its social arrangement, and in the manifold variety of its intellectual interests, none of which is unrepresented. It is therefore not presumptuous to hope that it will increasingly satisfy the just requirements of the country;

and that the Founder himself would allow
that the vineyard which he planted so gene-
rously, and fenced in with such parental care,
is bearing no wild grapes, but such a solid

TYTHE BARN

fruitage as could be gathered from no merely
modern garden.

Oxford is a place of visions and of dreams,
which float about, but do not encumber, the
earnest life of the present. Let us resume
our first corner of observation, and before

we pass out through the gateway by which
we entered, allow a few of the many sights
which the precincts of these grey walls
have witnessed to pass before our mental
eyesight. We see the early preparations
for the establishment; the fourteenth century Bishop and his agents viewing the
various plots of ground, selecting, rejecting,
bargaining; the jury of good men and true
treading the somewhat rough and unsavoury
site, and passing shrewd remarks upon it,
deciding in the end that the City would be
no loser by its appropriation. Then the
first stone is laid, the wise-hearted Master
Mason appears with his assistant craftsmen,
and the great idea is turned into a greater
reality, a fabric with foundations, and reared
upon a scale which Oxford had not yet
known. The great day of the formal
entry comes, the solemn procession, the
settling into the stately home and the
ordered life, followed by many generations
of still and scholarly increase, after the
Founder was himself withdrawn by death.
Many visitors, from many lands, come to
visit the new College; the lords and others
of the King's Council in 1388, the Duke
of Lancaster, Wykeham's old enemy, in
1393 (who is sumptuously entertained
with comfits and wine, and doubtless
with other "epulae lautiores"), Cardinal
Beaufort, the Visitor, in 1399. For an
incident in the change from the old to
the new learning we must turn to the

original record (a report by Dr. Layton to King Henry VIII. of a visitation of the University) :—

"In New College we have established a lecturer in Greek and another in Latin with an honest salary and stipend. . . . Wee have set Dunce (Duns Scotus) in Bocardo (*i.e.* in prison), and have utterly banished him Oxford for ever, with all his blynd glosses, and is now made a common servant to every man, fast nayled up upon posts. . . . And the second time wee came to New College, after wee had declared your injunctions, wee found all the great Quadrant Court full of the leaves of Dunce, the wind blowing them into every quarter; and there wee found one Master Greenefeld, a Gentleman of Buckinghamshire, gathering up part of the said book-leaves (as he said) therewith to make Sewells or Blanshers to keepe the Deere within the wood, and thereby to have the better crye with his hounds."

Absit omen ! we piously murmur, and pass on. We will close our eyes on the stern realities of the Reformation struggle, though they may never be forgotten. Too soon come the alarm of war, and war itself, with sights and sounds new to a College quadrangle; the train-bands exercising, the Cloisters stored with ammunition, the engineers at work upon the walls; and once and again the apparition of a Court and its vanities. When things quiet down, a long, and possibly dull, reign of shovel-hats, periwigs, and gaiters follows, in which an outside crust of formality did much to smother intellectual activity, yet beneath it room was found for a generous common life of scholarship, and wit, and literary pursuits. The less pompous but somewhat prim days of the later Hanoverian kings found some rugged eccentric figures still lingering in College Courts, the counterparts of the "men unscoured" whom the poet Wordsworth [1] marked in his undergraduate days among the Fellows of a great society on the Cam. It must have been good to hear among them the resonant and mirth-compelling laugh of the "Athenian Carter." Stiffness gradually relaxes as we move on to the later Victorian era; and now the College begins to become populous with the multitude of incomers, and its active connection with the University and the country passes into a new phase. To many the spectacle of February 3, 1903, is indelibly associated with these venerable buildings, and with it we may suitably conclude our musings. Upon that day Warden Sewell was laid to rest in the Cloisters, in the presence of an immense concourse of members of the College, and of representatives of the University and of the sister Colleges. With him were gathered up the memories of more than eighty years,

---

[1] "Prelude," book iii.

the earlier of them shared by none or by
very few of those whom he left behind,
while those of nearly fifty years belong to
that era of modern development, which
will be associated hereafter with his name,
and in which he bore the part of a loyal
and equitable ruler.

Such visions of the past may be the
dreams which old men are allowed to
dream; but how many visions of the future
have been granted to young men within
these courts and gardens; dreams which
may have been the inspiration of a great
career, or the memory of which may have
soothed the regrets for imperfect fulfilment.
There has been the scholar's aspiration,
sometimes realised even beyond hope, sometimes lost later on "in the light of common
day," sometimes buried in an early grave,
over which might be written in sad earnest
the words of the English scholar-poet :
"Literarum quæsivit gloriam, videt Dei."
To many in the older time the dream may
have taken a concrete form which had its
limitations, perhaps of the College living
which had been the expected portion from
tender years, yet it too touched with hope,
and the desire for usefulness, and often
with romance. The modern dream perhaps has had larger outlines, forecasting
great service to be done for God and man,
the command of the attention of senates or
courts, a man's share in the white man's
burden by the Indus or the Nile. These

dreams do not clog the life and work of the present ; they have arisen, as they always will arise, out of the consciousness of powers newly realised, and of opportunities here freely offered and gratefully embraced, before the waking vision of many

> " Who, rowing hard against the stream,
> Saw distant gates of Eden gleam,
> And did not dream it was a dream."

INDEX

97   G

INDEX

INDEX

THE END

For EU product safety concerns, contact us at Calle de José Abascal, 56–1°,
28003 Madrid, Spain or eugpsr@cambridge.org.

www.ingramcontent.com/pod-product-compliance
Ingram Content Group UK Ltd.
Pitfield, Milton Keynes, MK11 3LW, UK
UKHW012337130625
459647UK00009B/348